Animalographies
Spidernaut
Arabella, the Spider in Space

Jodie Parachini　　　illustrated by **Dragan Kordić**

Albert Whitman & Company
Chicago, Illinois

For Mommus and Popsie—JP

To Maša—DK

Library of Congress Cataloging-in-Publication data is on file with the publisher.

Text copyright © 2021 by Jodie Parachini

Illustrations copyright © 2021 by Albert Whitman & Company

Illustrations by Dragan Kordić

First published in the United States of America in 2021 by Albert Whitman & Company

ISBN 978-0-8075-0441-3 (hardcover) • ISBN 978-0-8075-0440-6 (ebook)

Printed in China

10 9 8 7 6 5 4 3 2 1 WKT 26 25 24 23 22 21

Design by Aphelandra

For more information about Albert Whitman & Company,

visit our website at www.albertwhitman.com.

Weaving a web is hard work.
I should know; I've had to do it
on Earth *and* in space.

I'm Arabella, the spidernaut.

Spiders in space may sound like science fiction, but my story is true. Back in 1972, a high school student named Judith Miles thought up an amazing experiment, and the astronauts at NASA thought it was pretty amazing too.

Judith wanted to know if a spider could spin a web in space.
Spinning a web is tricky. Common, orb-weaving cross spiders like
me make webs that look delicate but have to be strong enough for
us to walk on without breaking. We decide how to spin our webs
based on how much we weigh. But in space we would weigh…
you guessed it…NOTHING. That's because there is zero gravity
in space, which is why astronauts look like they're floating.

Can spiders weave webs in space? was such a great question that NASA decided to send my friend Anita and me into space.

We won't be the first insects or animals in space—there were fruit flies, mice, frogs, dogs, and monkeys before us—but none of those animals know how to spin webs, so our experiment is unique.

We will travel up to Skylab 3—a space station launched into Earth's orbit by the United States in 1973—along with three astronauts: Owen Garriott, Alan Bean, and Jack Lousma.

WEB DIARY 🕸 **JULY 25, 1973**

Think of it—me, an arachnid (a scientific name for spiders), just minding my own business one day and then—Spidernaut! I'm going to follow in the footsteps of some of the great space animals before me, like Laika the dog and Ham the chimp. Maybe someday, people will remember my name too!

The moment has arrived! On July 28, we're given a huge dinner. Common spiders can live for three weeks without food, but this trip is going to last fifty-six days, so I hope they don't forget the snacks!

Then we're put into vials that look like long tubes. There's only room in here for a watery sponge (for me to drink from), an extra dead fly (just in case), and me. No room to spin webs in here. Think of these vials like our own private rocket ships—for takeoff and landing.

Strap in, Spidernauts! 3...2...1...We have liftoff!

It was a bumpy ride aboard the Saturn 1B rocket that
took us to Skylab, and the trip took more than eight hours,
but we made it.

WEB DIARY  **AUGUST 5, 1973**

I'm in space! I feel woozy. I can't tell whether I'm right side up or upside down. The astronaut who's taking care of me, Owen, tried to get me to leave my tube today, but I didn't want to. It looks scary out there, all dark and...spacey. None of my eight legs seem to be able to grab onto anything. I wonder whether Anita likes this feeling. This was NOT what I was expecting.

Owen finally had to thump my tube to get me out.
Ooof! Look at me, I'm floating!

Here I am, in the cage. Home sweet home.
The cage reminds me of a window frame.
It's where I'll be spinning my web, *if I can*.

DAY 1

Now here's the big question:

How am I supposed to spin a web when there's nothing to attach it to?

And why does it feel like none of my legs works?

Owen called it "moving erratically in a swimming motion."

Have you ever seen a spider swimming? In space?
More like flailing.

I don't think it's possible to make a web here.

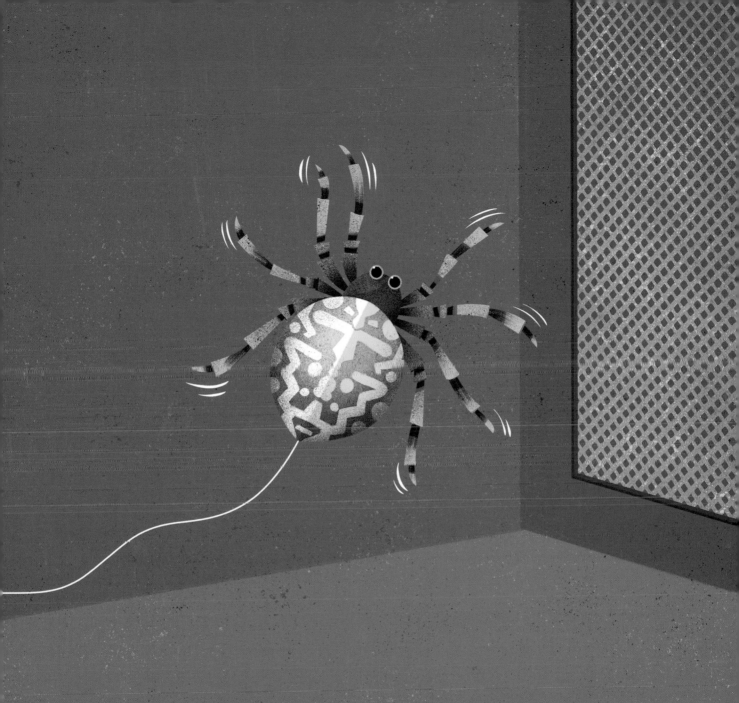

DAY 2

Still swimming. Actually, this isn't so bad.
There's no up or down, but I'm starting to get the
hang of this. This mesh screen on the cage walls might
be an okay place for a web. Maybe I'll give it a try.

WEB DIARY  AUGUST 7, 1973

Well, I did it—but it was terrible. My first web in space was a shaky, zigzaggy failure. I usually pride myself on making beautiful, neat circles, but not today. This wonky web has to go—it's just a mess of silk with more holes than strands. I guess I'll have to eat it and start again. (Yes, eat it. That's what we spiders do.) Web silk is made of protein, which I'll need for energy if I'm going to try again tomorrow.

DAY 3

My second web was much better. Web making is serious business. Spiders make a different kind of silk for each part of our webs.

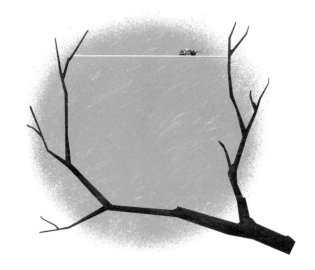

I start by making a bridge with really strong silk. It has to be strong because the whole web will hang from the bridge.

Next, I make the outside frame using nonsticky silk because it needs to support me, not to help me catch a meal.

Then I add the radials—like
spokes on a bicycle wheel.

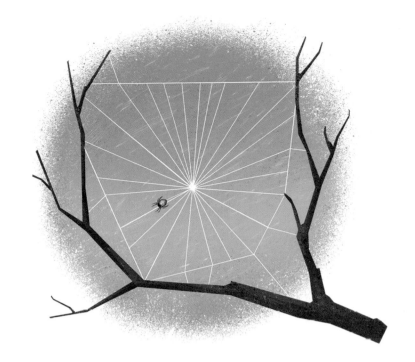

When everything's perfect, I can switch to
the sticky silk and start on my circles. *Voila!*

It took me quite a few days, but I've finally made a decent web. And I was the first spider ever to spin a web in zero gravity! That makes me a Guinness World Records award winner.

Spiders use webs for trapping and storing food. Up here, however, I will never catch a fly—nobody told me there aren't any insects flying around Skylab 3! Good thing the astronauts brought a container of dead ones. I think Owen has taken a liking to me, though, because instead of feeding me dead flies, he's requested a change to the experiment so he can give us bits of rare filet mignon (that's a fancy steak). Owen also took pictures and collected some of my webs to bring back to Earth for scientists to examine.

Owen studied me for three weeks and then, on August 26,
it's Anita's turn. Like me, she doesn't want to leave the vial at first
and even clings onto Owen's arm before being placed in the cage.
But she adapts really well to being in space and can spin her web
even quicker than I did—a whole day faster. Her reaction to
being weightless is recorded on camera and videotape.

Here are some of the cool discoveries scientists find from our experiment:

- ✺ First, scientists wanted to study a spider's central nervous system (that's the network made up of the brain and nerve clusters, and in humans, the spinal cord, which controls body movements). Studying our movements and how our brains reacted to the lack of gravity helped researchers examine how different medicines and drugs might affect the *human* nervous system.

- ✺ Scientists found that spiders need to get used to near-weightlessness before we can spin a good web. Even though we're born knowing how to spin webs, Anita and I had to get used to our surroundings before we could start.

Our webs in space were about the same shapes as on Earth but the silk was finer, probably because the webs didn't need to support our weight. The silk in our Earth webs is the same thickness all around but, in space, some parts are thinner, maybe because we start and stop spinning more often, to figure out where to put the threads. On Earth, gravity and wind help us do that.

WEB DIARY ⬟ AUGUST 26, 1973

I know my silk is tougher than steel (it's true!) and much more stretchy and elastic, but who knew that I would change it based on gravity? I'm so amazed and proud that I was selected for this adventure. And even if I never set eight legs back down on land again, it has been an honor to have been part of this fact-finding mission.

On September 25, our mission ended. Astronaut Owen brought the samples of our amazing webs back to NASA after our nearly two-month trip aboard Skylab 3. Judith (remember her—the student who thought up this experiment in the first place) was invited to the Marshall Space Flight Center in Huntsville, Alabama, to examine the webs and photographs. Lucky girl!

None of the astronauts knew what effect the experiment would have on us or our life spans, which is usually about one year. Neither Anita nor I survived long enough to be a part of any further space explorations, but I'm super proud to have been one of the first spidernauts in space. Since us, there have been more:

🕸 Two orb-weaving spiders nicknamed Elmo and Spiderman were launched aboard the Space Shuttle *Endeavour* on November 14, 2008, to visit the International Space Station. The project allowed students on Earth to compare the habits of the spiders in space to those kept in their classrooms.

A few years later, from May 16 to July 21, 2011, teachers and students on Earth watched video links following two golden orb spiders, Esmerelda and Gladys, as they adapted to life aboard the International Space Station. The videos even showed Esmerelda capturing a live fruit fly provided by the astronauts, adding a new twist to spidernaut experiments.

Another student project in 2012 sent Nefertiti, a Johnson jumping spider, to the International Space Station. Jumping spiders don't spin webs to catch prey—they leap! Nefertiti lived for one hundred days in space and made it home again.

Being a spidernaut was a great experience—especially knowing that our experiments helped astronauts (and the students back home who were cheering us on) study and learn about spiders in space.

That's one small step for man but one giant leap for spiders!

SPIDER FACTS

Cross spiders, or European garden spiders, are known as orb-weaving spiders because of the spiral, or circular, shapes of their webs (*orb* refers to a circle or sphere). The *cross* in their name comes from the white markings or dots that form a cross pattern on the back of their abdomen. They can range in color from yellow and orange to brown and gray, and range in size from 0.2 to 0.8 inches. The female is usually larger than the male.

HABITAT

Cross spiders live throughout North America and Europe. They particularly like gardens, fields, meadows, woodlands, and forests, but they can also be found in urban areas, especially in window frames and door frames. They eat mainly flying insects, like mosquitoes, wasps, and flies (and rarely, filet mignon steak). Their bite is painful but harmless to humans.

WEB BUILDING

Cross spiders build webs to catch their prey. Any flying insect caught in the web will be given a paralyzing bite, wrapped in silk thread, and eaten.

ARABELLA AND ANITA

Unfortunately, Anita died in space on September 16, 1973, and was returned to her vial. Arabella died some time during the return flight to Earth, around September 25. Both spiders showed signs of dehydration, a loss of too much of their body fluids.

WHERE ARE THEY NOW?

Arabella was preserved, along with samples of her webs, and transferred from NASA to the Smithsonian National Air and Space Museum in Washington, DC, in 1974. Anita is on display in the space science exhibit at the Steven F. Udvar-Hazy Center in Chantilly, Virginia.